MORGAN DUZOGLOU & ROBERT DUZOGLOU

Life Quest

A Transformational
Journey

BALBOA.
PRESS
A DIVISION OF HAY HOUSE

Balboa Press books may be ordered through booksellers or by contacting:

Balboa Press
A Division of Hay House
1663 Liberty Drive
Bloomington, IN 47403
www.balboapress.com
1 (877) 407-4847

Because of the dynamic nature of the Internet, any web addresses or links contained in this book may have changed since publication and may no longer be valid. The views expressed in this work are solely those of the author and do not necessarily reflect the views of the publisher, and the publisher hereby disclaims any responsibility for them.

The author of this book does not dispense medical advice or prescribe the use of any technique as a form of treatment for physical, emotional, or medical problems without the advice of a physician, either directly or indirectly. The intent of the author is only to offer information of a general nature to help you in your quest for emotional and spiritual well-being. In the event you use any of the information in this book for yourself, which is your constitutional right, the author and the publisher assume no responsibility for your actions.

Any people depicted in stock imagery provided by Getty Images are models, and such images are being used for illustrative purposes only.
Certain stock imagery © Getty Images.

Print information available on the last page.

This book is a work of non-fiction. Unless otherwise noted, the author and the publisher make no explicit guarantees as to the accuracy of the information contained in this book and in some cases, names of people and places have been altered to protect their privacy.

ISBN: 978-1-5043-9907-4 (sc)
ISBN: 978-1-5043-9909-8 (hc)
ISBN: 978-1-5043-9908-1 (e)

Library of Congress Control Number: 2018902524

Balboa Press rev. date: 03/02/2018

Contents

To the most remarkable father a person could ask for. Your soul is exemplary, your discipline is unparalleled, your kindness and generosity are infinite, and the sacrifices you have made and continue to make for your family and those you care for are the sole reason we have the opportunities and blessings that we do. You have united us, strengthened us, filled us with your wisdom, and infused us with an unconditional love that will last our families for generations to come. You are a true king among men. There is no honor grand enough to encompass all that you mean to us.

Preface

Congratulations are in order! You've arrived at your moment—a time when you have decided to quest, discover, and experience more for your life, body, mind, and soul.

Now, where to start? This can be an overwhelming and daunting task if not approached correctly, so first things first. Take a deep breath, and make sure you are here, present, in the now, and in an "in-lightened" state of being.

Let's begin by explaining what *Life Quest* is all about. *Life Quest* is your personal map to navigate your life! This map is written for you, by you, the seeker, who has a burning desire to move past the obvious and beyond this drone mentality that so many have adopted; who feels in your soul that there is so much more to life than what you are currently experiencing. *You* have the desire and hold the possibilities to uncover and pursue your God-given and undeniable truth.

As a collective we have made tremendous strides in various fields—medicine, science, technology, etc. However, as *you* have most likely noticed, our progress in consciousness has come to a standstill—in some cases, deteriorated—and is now retreating at a rapid pace. We have become externally in touch, yet internally out of touch. The honor and respect of the self, Mother Nature, family, and humankind has given way to an immense and self-centered desire to advance and to overindulge ourselves. These misguided advances have become today's standard way of living.

Luckily you're not satisfied, you're not a drone, and you most certainly are not willing to settle for an unexceptional existence, are you? That's why you're here. *Life Quest* is designed to bring clarity and direction to your personal journey; to empower you to breach the bonds that bind you; to liberate and assist you in living your life with a powerful purpose. Welcome ... welcome to the expansive possibilities of the rest of your life. Are you ready? Let's do this!

Acknowledgments

Life Quest is a work of miracles that came to fulfillment due to a tremendous amount of love, support, dedication, direction, and knowledge.

First and most important, we are eternally grateful to God for allowing this powerful message of light to shine through and touch each reader who embodies its message. Thanks to Lori Duzoglou, for your boundless motherly energy and abundant support, and to Derek Duzoglou, for your keen eye and attention to detail every step of the way. And since we are only as strong as the shoulders we stand upon, we would like to give our humble and most sincere thanks to our united family of mentors, guides, and angels. To become as you are would be life's greatest quest.

Introduction

This is your moment. Your time. Your unique journey in finding yourself. Your gifts and your purpose. *Life Quest* will guide you through a process of discovery. An adventure! You are going to become very aware of yourself in many different capacities, and as a result, your perspectives will most certainly take a shift for the grander.

Finding balance among your body, mind, and soul is primary in moving forward and optimizing your advancement. In order to achieve balance, however, searching and understanding must first occur. With these skills gifted specifically for your unique journey, you will learn the value, function, and connection of each of them. You will be accessing external energy as well as looking internally for many of your answers, as you already hold the definite key. *Life Quest* will assist you in unlocking the treasure that will lead to unlimited possibilities.

The divine connection, mind-set, attitude, and tools that you will unleash with *Life Quest* are not momentary or stagnant. They will serve as a detailed map, a compass for you to live by for as long as you please. The peace that comes with the connection and balance of this trinity is tangible. It sets the tone for you to live an "in-lightened" life.

Get ready to delve deep, to search every corner of your body, mind, and soul to discover your ultimate truth and purpose. You'll answer questions, attack tasks, create new mind-sets, access internal and external energy, journal, and much more. The DNA of your being and your purpose is unique to you and only you. If not yearned for or searched for, it may lie dormant just under your surface, and your potential may never be realized. As your captain on this magnificent ship of life, *Life Quest* will work together with you to find the grand possibility that is already you. Open yourself to the promise of fulfillment, love, connection, balance, happiness, and so much more. Uncover your treasure before it's lost!

Life Quest can't wait to introduce you to the marvel that is *you!*

1

Re-Member the Three

The three great reinforcements that have been granted to you for your adventurous life journey are your body, mind, and soul. Your first step is to take a close look and initiate the recognition of these titans. How many times have you heard these three linked? A countless number, I'm sure. But what significance have you given to them? They are as limited or expansive as the intentions, sentiments, and efforts you place behind them. They are the keys to unlocking and opening the door of possibilities.

Checkpoint: Starting Point
Write down what each of these powerhouses means to you. No need for a grand story; simply write the first thought that comes to mind. The first thought that comes to you while in a calm state is typically the purest. These pure thoughts are the lights that you reflect when you're connected.

Body: _____

_____

_____

Mind: _____

_____

_____

Soul: _____

_____

_____

Your words above have power. Words, thoughts, and intentions give energy and power to your aspirations, allowing you to bring them to fruition. Your words will manifest themselves into your actions, and these actions are what turn general, mindless motion into pointed habits and deeds. These pointed habits and deeds are you living in your purpose and forming your legacy. Your body, mind, and soul are the means necessary for your words to take form for you. Manifested, they become your dreams, fears, and desires.

Now that you have clearly written your interpretation of this trinity and what they mean to you, you can continue on your journey.

The reason that re-member is used in the title is because that is exactly what you are doing with the big three. You are re-membering to their all-encompassing and expansive power in your life. You are reconnecting to them. As beings in this modern world, it can be very easy to lose sight of this connection. When born, we are instinctively keen on when we need to eat or sleep (body). At a young age, we are alert and process new information at the highest rate in our lives (mind), and we are connected to (and intuitive of) many energies (soul). With the exercise above, your *Life Quest* journey begins the process in which you are re-membering to this way of being in a bigger, brighter, and more powerful way. Re-member to your gifts, being, and purpose.

By highlighting and focusing on these factors, you start to convert the way you move through your life, as well as transforming the purpose behind your movement. The activity above is your benchmark and orientation of your journey, a circuit that will shine brighter and strengthen as you continually focus and work on it.

2

Balance

Continuing after your wonderful process of re-membering, your next key step is to understand the balance between the body, mind, and soul. To obtain a fluid balance between each of them at a very high vibration is imperative to fulfilling your purpose. This cannot be accomplished if you are neglected or in hyperactive overdrive. Balance and optimization are skills you will begin to address during this process. It's a difficult task that will challenge you immensely, but you already knew that. The payoff is priceless, but you already knew that too. It's time for you to re-member that instinctive knowledge. You see? You're already on your way.

Checkpoint: Benchmarks
Continue to benchmark and evaluate your current position. What you measure you can manage. On a scale from one to ten (one being the least and ten being optimal), answer the following:

Body: How much focused developmental effort do you dedicate to your body?

_____

Mind: How much focused developmental effort do you dedicate to your mind?

_____

Soul: How much focused developmental growth do you dedicate to your soul?

_____

Body

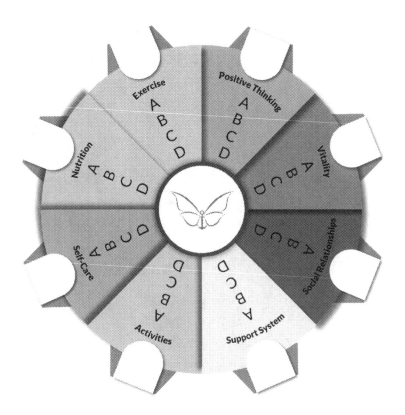

Mind

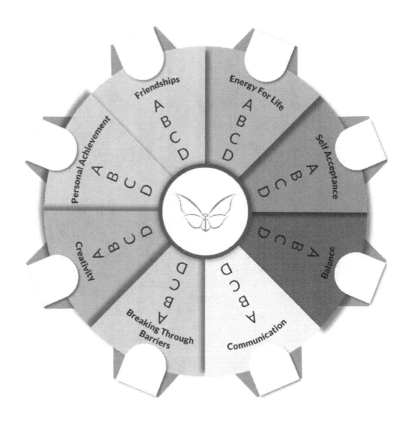

Soul/Spirituality

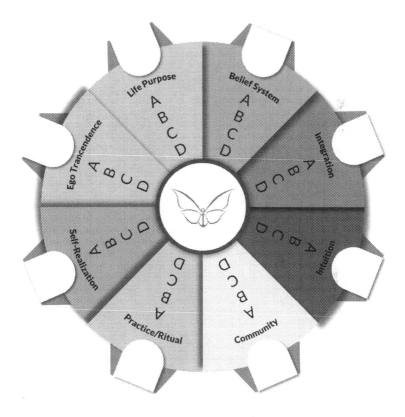

The crucial information you have evaluated about yourself sheds more light on your foundation and how to better reinforce it.

3

Thought Pattern

The incredible expanding mind! Let's shed some light and power on it.

The mind spends its time performing two great functions. Yes, you read correctly—just two:

1. Analyzing threat
2. Capitalizing on opportunity

Take a second to mull this over. This concept is so simple, yet simultaneously complex that we almost feel as if some mind-boggling explanation is missing. Yet it's not. Interesting, right? The mind is the ultimate computer. I'll even go as far as to call it the best survival computer. Anywhere from forty thousand to sixty thousand thoughts are generated by our minds each day from the moment we open our eyes to the second we fall asleep at night. All those thoughts are focused on the two themes listed above. As a matter of fact, a large handful of them are repeated over and over again to remind us what we need to do to survive and thrive. Understanding the process and patterns repeated by our minds is key to being able to better capitalize on the mind's brilliance and not fall victim to its delusions. One of your most important goals will be to direct your thoughts.

Checkpoint: Get to Know Yourself
Write down one predominant thought that repeats itself daily. Try to get to the root of this thought.

Thought: _____

_____

_____

_____

Wonderful! Now let's go deeper. There are three main themes in thought pattern. The first is called *casual thought*. This thought comes into focus as fast as it goes out. This thought is random and as plentiful as the stars in the sky, and it fills much of every paused moment.

The second type of thought is *observant thought*. This thought studies your surroundings and experiences, constantly observing, evaluating, and filing into categories—compartmentalizing, if you will.

And last is the thought you deliberately searched for and wrote down above. This is *driving thought*. It is charged with energy and emotion, both positive and negative. Driving thought shapes your life to a great extent. If you study this thought, you will understand its intensity. This is the reason it pushed its way to the surface when you looked.

Caution Bubble

There is a danger here if you're not careful. The danger is making the mind your master, allowing it to run and control your entire existence. Your goal here is to take control and responsibility of the operator/programmer, and make sure the mind is assisting—not ruling and running—your quest. Remember that your mind is only one leg of your circuit.

An overactive mind either will constantly and tirelessly seek problems, which will slowly turn into fear, or will become tyrannical and seizing in order to fulfill its insensible and insatiable desire to win, grow, and/or fix everything.

4

Mind's Eye

Now that you've begun to study your mind, you slowly will reveal other abilities that you possess. This observer who is studying your thoughts is the one we will bring to the forefront, understanding, empowering, and balancing with the other two great assistants, your body and your soul. Remember you are more than just your thoughts.

As you begin to expose your thought process, it's important to consistently eliminate harmful thoughts. Don't give them power over your life. This process is a lifelong discipline with tremendous benefits. You will eventually see these thoughts coming a mile away, and with this new knowledge, understanding, and capacity, you will be able to quickly dispose of them.

Checkpoint: Positive and Negative Mind Observation/ Training
There are three steps to this checkpoint. Each step guides you in observing your thoughts and gives you pointed insight as to your mind's strengths and weaknesses.

Step 1: Write down three persistent positive (P) and three persistent negative (N) thoughts.

P _____

P _____

P _____

N _____

N _____

N _____

Step 2: Write down the way each of the thoughts affects you. (How do you feel, act, react, and so on?)

P _____

P _____

P _____

N _____

N _____

N _____

Step 3: Write down three ways to recognize and eliminate negative thoughts.

1. _____

_____

_____

2. _____

_____

_____

3. _____

_____

_____

5

In-Lightened

Remember that play on words from the preface: "in-lightened"? Let me explain. Living in an "in-lightened" state of being means that you are *in light*! You experience what it is to be in your highest vibration. You allow your joyous self to shine through, you feel and breathe, and you are in peace and purpose. Too often, we are so affected by certain surroundings, circumstances, and daily grinds that we forget to live true to ourselves and what makes us uniquely—well—us. We forget to be in our light. You're most certainly feeling the urge to reach this state at this stage of your quest.

When our minds are in *enlightened* states, it leads to extraordinary experiences and produces more than satisfying outcomes. Now is when you must take a very close look at yourself and where you are in this very moment. This self-analysis provides you with a map of your thought process, personality, and value system. Know with complete certainty that this information is imperative for your growth and is of extreme value. What you're learning about yourself may even surprise you.

Caution Bubble

Looking inside yourself can be scary. You may not like what you see in yourself at first. Let me tell you—inside—that's where the sugar is, honey! In Life Quest, there are no excuses, no faults, and no right or wrong answers. There is only understanding, forward motion, and growth into the amazing potential that you are unleashing.

Checkpoint: Self-Analysis

Breathe, take your time, and let go. The more honest you are with yourself, the more it will help prepare you to move forward.

Describe yourself in one word.

_____

If you stand for only one value, what is it (for example, truth, honor, and so on)?

_____

What three adjectives would you use to describe yourself at your best?

1. _____

2. _____

3. _____

What three adjectives would you use to describe yourself at your worst?

1. _____

2. _____

3. _____

What three adjectives would people who know you use to describe you at your best?

1. _____

2. _____

3. _____

What three adjectives would people who know you use to describe you at your worst?

1. _____

2. _____

3. _____

List ten of your top values (e.g., loyalty, family, health, and so on).
Rate each one of your values on a scale of one to ten, based on their importance to you.
Rate each one of your values on a scale of one to ten, based on their currently lived and active relevance.

Value	Importance	Lived/Active
1. _____	_____	_____
2. _____	_____	_____
3. _____	_____	_____

4. _____   _____   _____

5. _____   _____   _____

6. _____   _____   _____

7. _____   _____   _____

8. _____   _____   _____

9. _____   _____   _____

10. _____   _____   _____

List three things that you love the most.

1. _____

2. _____

3. _____

List three things that anger you the most.

1. _____

2. _____

3. _____

List three thoughts that motivate you.

1. _____

2. _____

3. _____

List three thoughts that hold you back.

1. _____

2. _____

3. _____

List three thoughts that help you.

1. _____

2. _____

3. _____

List three thoughts that hurt you.

1. _____

2. _____

3. _____

List three thoughts that are constantly active in your mind.

1. _____

2. _____

3. _____

List three thoughts that you wish to let go of.

1. _____

2. _____

3. _____

List a strong thought of your past.

_____

_____

_____

List a strong thought of your present.

_____

_____

_____

List a strong thought you have of your future.

_____

_____

_____

What three changes do most want to make in your life?

1. _____

2. _____

3. _____

What three actions do most want to take in your life?

1. _____

2. _____

3. _____

What is your strongest desire for your life?

_____

_____

_____

_____

What is your philosophy?

_____

_____

_____

_____

What is your purpose?

_____

_____

_____

_____

Rate each area of your life so that you may truly understand where you are satisfied, where you are unsatisfied, and what you have to do to become a balanced being.

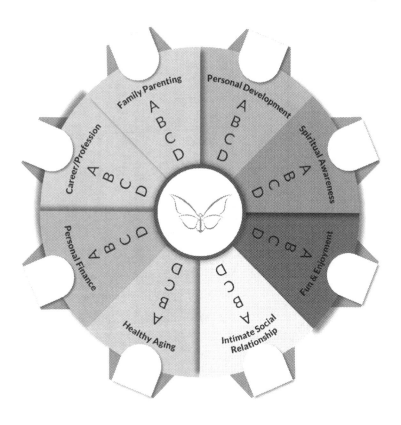

6

Core Values Assessment

Let's add a bit to the extensive internal work that you're doing, shall we?

Having a core value system is a practice for a well-rounded and balanced person. You've already written down ten of your most important values above, but what about those in second or third place? They may become at the top of your list one day. Just because a few of them may slip your mind or not be as relevant at the moment doesn't mean that you should look past them entirely. Better to have them ripe and ready for when you choose to put them into action.

Checkpoint

Rate each core value on a scale of one to ten, based on its importance in your life. Then rate each core value on a scale of one to ten, based on how well you live each value (or how well you "walk the talk")

Core Value	Importance 1–10	Lived 1–10
Accomplishment		
Abundance		

Achievement   _____   _____

Adventure   _____   _____

Beauty   _____   _____

Clarity   _____   _____

Commitment   _____   _____

Communication   _____   _____

Community   _____   _____

Connecting to Others _____   _____

Creativity   _____   _____

Emotional Health   _____   _____

Environment   _____   _____

Excellence   _____   _____

Family   _____   _____

Flexibility   _____   _____

Freedom   _____   _____

Friendship   _____   _____

Fulfillment   _____   _____

Fun   _____   _____

Holistic Living   _____   _____

Honesty   _____   _____

Humor   _____   _____

Integrity   _____   _____

Joy   _____   _____

Leadership   _____   _____

Loyalty   _____   _____

Nature   _____   _____

Openness   _____   _____

Orderliness   _____   _____

Personal Growth   _____   _____

Partnership   _____   _____

Physical Appearance   _____   _____

Power   _____   _____

Privacy   _____   _____

Professionalism   _____   _____

Recognition   _____   _____

Respect   _____   _____

Romance   _____   _____

Security   _____   _____

Self-Care   _____   _____

Self-Expression   _____   _____

Self-Mastery   _____   _____

Self-Realization   _____   _____

Sensuality   _____   _____

Service   _____   _____

Spirituality   _____   _____

Trust   _____   _____

Vitality   _____   _____

Walking the Talk   _____   _____

7

In-Sight

"In-sight"—the brilliance of this! The process and exercises that you have been performing have propelled you forward and upward. You are now at the stage where you see your mind from an observer's standpoint. Your mind is quite literally *in sight*. You now clearly can understand that your thoughts are an integral part of who you are, yet these thoughts do not complete or define you, nor are they your complete makeup. Knowing this, understanding this, and using this is a new mental step for your growth.

As you observe your mind, you will find that the thoughts of your experiences are a map of your journey—your life's imprint on your experience of past, present, and future. This map is to be honored and respected, as it is what has guided you to now. Even the most painful and profound thoughts you may have are vital in how they shape your mental realm. Every encounter, every memory, every experience is carefully recorded and cataloged for your future reference. Never doubt that your mind is ready and willing to assist you in the next challenge of your growth.

Caution Bubble

Beware! More often than not, people think they have to completely forget their previous experiences in order to move forward. This philosophy couldn't be further from the truth. Embrace your past—the good, the bad, and the ugly. These experiences give you a reference point. They allow you to know what you want and don't want for your present and future. Respect the thoughts of your past. These are the very moments that will build your character and will give you certain strengths and wisdom you may not even know you possess.

Now that you're paying attention to your mind's function, you'll find that your mind analyzes and judges every moment as either dangerous or adventurous and threatening or helpful for you. This most certainly sounds like a good companion to have on a quest. With this grounding and direction, you begin to establish a reliable foundation.

As mentioned earlier, life is experienced in three dimensions: the body, the mind, and the soul. The mind is the linear demarcation of these three—the timeline, the history, the learned and adopted benchmarks of your life. The resources that the mind provides are bountiful yet a bit limiting, as this is only one of the three dimensions. Without the realm of the body and the soul working in tandem, the mind's possibilities are confined to an accounting ledger of plus and minus. In actuality, without the body and soul accompanying the mind, your experience would be only partial and confined.

8

Limit-Less

Due to the mind's linear dimensions there can be a danger of limiting progress. As creatures of habit, we have a tendency to tie events and experiences together based on their familiarity or relation to previous similar exposure. Should an experience have brought difficulty, future correlated experiences may be avoided or acted upon with aggression. Your mind perceives these experiences as a threat. On the flip side, we have the pleasurable experiences. These can just as easily be a danger. If not tamed, they will more often than not drive you to abuse by desire or careless repetition.

Your mind's desire to catalog and judge in a hurry can sometimes lead it to overlook situations that may not be familiar to its previous experiences. The last thing you want is to become mechanical with your interactions. Not every experience will be the same as a previous one. Limit yourself less in these experiences. Allow your mind to experience this new moment, rather than rush to correlate it to your past. Your past can be your map but certainly not your compass! Pay attention and trade in your cleverness for wonderment. Live every moment!

Caution Bubble

The final caution in the realm of the mind is the mind's ability to be influenced by another person. The mind can very easily take another's explanation of any situation or experience and treat it as doctrine. Some influences are for your betterment, however some are communal influences that can be downright dangerous. Discover *your* truth.

Your goal here is to limit *less*. Create space in your mind, which allows you to process your thoughts in a manner that does not limit you. By limiting yourself less, you allow your mind to become strong yet flexible—an "in-lightened" being of thought.

Checkpoint: Identify Your Boundaries

Write down three positive thoughts that reoccur on a regular basis.

1. _____

2. _____

3. _____

Write down three dangerous thoughts that reoccur on a regular basis.

1. _____

2. _____

3. _____

Write down three things to which you are drawn in an intense way.

1. _____

2. _____

3. _____

Write down three people in your life who influence you for the better, and describe why.

1. _____

2. _____

3. _____

Write down three people in your life that influence you for the worse, and describe why.

1. _____

2. _____

3. _____

Write down three thoughts on which you've stood firm, yet these thoughts were changed due to the influence of people or experiences.

1. _____

_____

2. _____

_____

3. _____

_____

9

Notes

(This section is dedicated to your personal thoughts, feelings and growth.)

_____

_____

_____

_____

_____

_____

_____

_____

_____

Morgan Duzoglou & Robert Duzoglou

Morgan Duzoglou & Robert Duzoglou

_____

_____

_____

_____

_____

_____

_____

_____

_____

_____

_____

_____

_____

_____

_____

10

Create Your Cure

Most of us, at some point, have heard a doctor say that the best remedy for any type of illness is a positive attitude. Why? The answer is simply because with a healthy and positive mind, there are many wonderful and endless are possibilities. As a matter of fact, studies show that the mind is capable of self-healing the body, from a minor cut to severe diseases. This mind-set makes you a force to be reckoned with. Unfortunately, the same holds true for a negative mind. If you always assume the worst, attract negative thoughts, and live in this dark state, it is inevitable that terrible things probably will occur.

One single negative thought can become like a virus in your mind. Lucky you—you now know how to see such thoughts coming from a mile away. You now have the knowledge and power to search out these negative thoughts and eliminate them before they grow roots. You have control and discipline, and you can observe your mind as a whole. If this isn't powerful, I don't know what is!

Checkpoint: Techniques to Clear and Cleanse Your Mind
Let's talk about the different types of techniques you can use to clear and cleanse your mind. Since you are unique, you can choose whichever technique works best

for you. It's recommended that you try them all before you rule out any of them. Get creative—try to come up with your own methods.

Imaging
In your mind's eye, choose to focus on something that helps you battle negativity—for example, a warrior who fights alongside you and defends you. Keep this as the focal point when you feel under attack.

Material Objects
You have the innate ability to tie any random object to a thought, sentiment, or memory. Use this to your advantage. Surround yourself with all that reminds you of joy, happiness, love, or any special feeling that you'd like. This object can be a photograph, a keepsake from your travels, or even something that a loved one gave you. The sky's the limit.

Bodily Senses
Your senses are so important to your daily life. Why not use them to your advantage? Focus on what you can do to get them working for your benefit. Listen to music that puts you in that over-the-top happy mood. Cook a meal (or, if you're like me, order out), something that drives your taste buds wild in the most divine way. Wear cozy comfortable clothes at home. All of these actions engage your senses with simple pleasure, releasing dopamine, an organic neurotransmitter increased by "happy stimulants", into your brain, thus literally allowing you to be "high on life." Sometimes it's the little things that make the most difference in how we fight our battles. Allow your body to assist you.

Purpose

Stay focused on a positive purpose. This is one of Life Quest's most essential messages. There's nothing like having busy hands and a busy mind for a worthwhile purpose to keep you positive. Get off the fence and jump. You have important work to do!

11

Wonder-Full Body

A very basic description of our five senses would be that they are the body's functions. In the grander scheme, that description is just a glimpse at the marvelous capabilities of the body. Besides being tasked with your regular daily functions, your body is constantly engaged in questing for your dreams and purpose. Additionally, it's a wondrous instrument of divine energy, waiting to be tuned and played by none other than you.

In this modern world, we tend to be very vain and shallow when it comes to the body, concentrating solely on appearances and our peers' opinions of us. There is also a tendency to treat the body as an entertainment unit. Neither of these is a bad thing, but both are limiting. If not balanced with the other functions of the body, it can lead us down a path of waste, pain, illness, and abuse, among other things.

See, write, speak, move, express, discover, sense— these are just a few of the many marvelous abilities that the body can do for and with you. Have you ever thought of it that way? Cool, right? The body is your vehicle that houses your mind and your soul. It behooves you to take the best care of it as possible, and that means keeping all of your senses and functions in tip-top shape. More than anything, appreciate the gift that the body is.

Checkpoint: Body Function Analysis
When was the last time you exerted your body to the max and felt amazing afterward?

_____

When was the last time you had a complete checkup with a doctor, nutritionist, healer, or other health professional?

_____

When was the last time you wrote out a letter or a journal entry by hand?

_____

When was the last time you smelled something so divine that you remembered the aroma for days?

_____

When was the last time you experienced a vast, open space and tested your eyes' potential to see beyond their limit?

_____

When was the last time you went for a walk or hike in nature until your legs couldn't carry you anymore?

_____

When was the last time you laughed so hard that your stomach hurt, and you could barely breathe?

_____

The functions that must be trained and expressed are the subtle abilities of the body to sense the energies that approach it. In addition to this ability, your body can amplify energy within itself, as well as the energy that is received from any exterior source, such as the sun and moon, wind and ocean, and even the trees. You are a power plant of action, healing, and transformation. Your body is quite literally your translator into action of your mind and soul—a true phenomenon, if you ask me.

Caution Bubble

The danger of negative energy being amplified is that it can manifest in the body. A sniffle can turn into something much worse. This negative energy can go as far as to create severe depression, tumors, diseases, and so on. Be mindful of the type of energy your body is amplifying.

Checkpoint 2: Body Energy Enhancer

Should you choose to give your body an energy boost, the following short meditation is a great way to do so. You can be anywhere as long as you're in a calm state and without distraction. You may enjoy sharing this exercise with a friend or family member as well. Try being the guide and walking others through it once you've become comfortable with it yourself. Think how grand all this new knowledge of in-lightenment and in-sight is when you're sharing it. What a gift!

Relax, quiet your mind, and breathe three deep breaths. Make yourself present and in the now. Walk yourself through a descriptive checklist of your body, starting with the very top of your head and working your way down, slowly covering and halting at each point that comes to mind for you. Remind yourself to relax at this point, and release any pressure, tension, and/or stress in this area. From your eyes to your lower back to your toes, fit as much in as you can. You can envision light covering you and these areas. In-lighten them and awaken them.

12

Amplify Your Energy

Let's begin this chapter with a few questions and answers.

If you were to point to your mind, where would you point? To your forehead, most likely.

If you were to point to your soul or heart, where would you point? Probably to your chest.

If you were to point to your body's center, where would you point? This most certainly would be your body's center point—the stomach. This is the center of the body's universe, and it's commonly overlooked or ignored completely.

The truth is that this energy point performs miraculous tasks for you, and you can utilize this gift. This life force drives your actions, your healing, and your strength. This is your very own power plant, which absorbs energy and allows it to flow through you in its all-encompassing magnificence.

"I have butterflies in my stomach."

"I know because I can feel it in my gut."

I'm sure you've heard these phrases, but have you ever looked deeper to understand the meaning behind them? What you're feeling is energy. You can amplify this energy and put it to work within your body and in your daily life. This is the point in which you feel nerves, sense your intuition, and make predictions on how you feel about someone or a situation at first encounter. It's even the area where you procreate. This point of central energy in your body feels and experiences energy before the mind even has the chance to process and filter a situation. Pay attention!

The ability to recognize this center of energy and focus, solely on the feeling it gives you, is raw power. As mentioned, you can build this energy and even transfer it to and from your surroundings. Picture superhero characters. Nine times out of ten when their superpowers come to life, you see some sort of light or fire coming from their stomach or chest area. This *is* your very own superpower; use it!

Checkpoint: Get to Know Your Center

For your reference, a few names given to this point are as follows:

- Sacred heart
- Center
- Tan tien
- Kanji
- Gut
- Intuition

Write down three times in your life when your center point was triggered. If you are not sure, you can do so the next time you get excited, nervous, scared, or have an instinctive feeling about a situation or person. After paying close attention to this center of energy, you'll realize that it always has been there, and it always will guide you and help you along your life's quest.

1. _____

_____

_____

_____

2. _____

_____

_____

_____

3. _____

_____

_____

_____

Checkpoint 2: Strengthen Your Center

Sit in a comfortable meditative position. Breath in through your nose and expand your lungs fully, allowing the air to flow all the way down to your center point.

After holding the air there and allowing your gut to expand, exhale though your mouth. Imagine your center point filling with life, positive energy, direction, purpose, and anything else that you call into your life. Build your center, and feel the strength that comes from connecting to it, feeling it, and applying it.

13

Come-Pass

Ahhh, the soul—one of my favorite subjects to discuss.

Your soul has unique DNA—part individual and unique to only you, part connected to nature and those surrounding you, and part divine or eternal.

The individual aspect of your soul is that part that is in charge of your mission, vision, purpose, and journey. It's the part that is specific to only you and no one else. The best way to emphasize point this is to ask what you're really passionate about.

The connected aspect of your soul is the part that relates to creation—nature, other individuals, culture. Each person, regardless of his or her heritage, race, religion, or culture, is made of the same essence. We are all carbon-based. (So are plants!) You may feel right at home in the ocean, while others prefer the forest, and still others would choose a mountaintop. You are connecting to the soul energy that envelops all. You are connecting to the source, creation, an energy that lies partly outside of you and is more than just yourself. There's a peace that lies in that.

The divine aspect of your soul is your connection to God—most certainly a connection to a greater energy, the ethereal "more" that we all feel deep inside of us in our centers. (But you knew that, didn't you?) God, the universe, light, energy—we can even go with the *Avatar* mentality, and call it Eywa. This greatness is your playing field. It connects to you in order to guide you and fill you with hope, faith, compassion, and many more magnanimous sensations. It makes this journey, awareness, and transformation possible.

Just to put things into perspective, here's a little guide:

The body expresses itself in the *now*. It's constantly in a new state of being (experience).

The mind expresses itself in the past. It draws from knowledge and experience to create.

The soul speaks in the future. It's your immediate connection to the individual, to other connected beings (nature included), and to the higher divine energy. Your soul directly translates its connection to your body and mind simultaneously, in order to create a balance and a possibility.

Your soul is your compass or, as I like to say it, "come-pass." Whatever comes your way, know that it has come for a reason, and after it is experienced by the body, analyzed by the mind, and felt by the soul, it will pass, and then the cycle will begin again. The very moment of creation, what we know as the *now*, is when all of this comes together and forges a brilliant burst of energy. The result of this burst is the epitome of creation at its peak performance. The result is *you*—all that you are and all that you will become.

14

Notes

(This section is dedicated to your personal thoughts, feelings and growth.)

_____

_____

_____

_____

_____

_____

_____

_____

Morgan Duzoglou & Robert Duzoglou

_____

_____

_____

_____

_____

_____

_____

_____

_____

_____

_____

_____

_____

Morgan Duzoglou & Robert Duzoglou

15

Leap of Faith

"What if I fall?"

"Oh, but what if you fly?"

You've come to a point in your quest when you have an all-encompassing understanding of the body and the mind—their functions, abilities, limits, and greatness. You comprehend the importance of a positive mind and attitude, you can appreciate what the body actually does and its importance to your quest, and you're starting to grasp the vast topic of the soul, the third key.

Since you now have this knowledge, I want you to have the ability to expand beyond it as well, to have the capacity to step outside of yourself and observe your body and your mind; to take a leap of faith into your destiny, quest, and purpose. This is by no means a small feat.

This skill will be useful for you in many areas of your life. It will teach you patience. It will give you calmness and serenity when interacting with others. Most important, however, it will allow you to have an ongoing and open dialogue with yourself. You will hear what your body needs and what your mind is curious about or what it yearns for, as well as the sensitivity of your soul. This experience comes with an ease that you will find hard to live without once you've tasted the peace it brings to you and to those around you, with whom you interact regularly. Have faith, jump, and enjoy your new wings!

Checkpoint: Techniques—Connecting to Your Soul and Beyond

Grounding: Sit on the ground, cross-legged, with back straight, palms facing down, and your open fingers on the ground by your sides. Close your eyes. Breathe in through your nose and out through your mouth repeatedly— gently, smoothly, and naturally. Truly feel the heartbeat of the earth with all of your soul. Feel! Are you now out of your mind?

Make sure you're not going over your to-do list, thinking about someone or what your plans are for the weekend. Be empty-minded and soul-full.

Meditation:_Sit cross-legged, with back straight. Allow your pointer finger to touch your thumb, with your palms facing down on your knees. Breathe. Focus. Your thoughts here are your choice; just make sure they are not cascading thoughts for which you can't control the progression. Choose only one thought. Train the mind to be quiet and focused.

Love

16

Soul Savvy

A topic as ethereal as the soul can be very difficult to explain, let alone understand. So let's make you *soul savvy*, savvy?

In the silence of the mind is where the soul can be detected and experienced. It speaks gently and subtly. When in this silence, you'll feel that your soul is as smooth, steady, and consistent as a baby's heartbeat, the earth's rotation, or even a breathtaking sunrise or sunset. This is the part of you that is connected to the "Universe Wide Web" of creative energy. The string theory that many of us have heard about is not so far off here. Your soul has the ability to connect to all things with an infinite wisdom and understanding.

You may have had moments that you can't explain— déjà vu; speaking about something clearly when you didn't know you knew about the topic; the strong feeling that you know someone from the first glance into his or her eyes. These are soul experiences. Your soul has an eternal history and future. There is a specific connection to God that would take lifetimes of discovery in order to comprehend, yet we can still have that moment when we are drawn to it and experience it.

Checkpoint: Your Soul Experiences
Now that you know what they are and how to identify them, write down three times that you've had a powerful soul experience.

1. _____

_____

_____

2. _____

_____

_____

3. _____

_____

_____

These soul experiences speak to you on a much deeper vibration than thoughts. Pay attention, listen, and allow yourself to feel these experiences to the fullest. In love, you can feel this, and when I say "in love," I mean living in love—with yourself, with your life, and with your surroundings; in a state of gratitude. In a state of love and gratitude, you are in a very high vibration, and your connection and balance with your mind, body, and soul are evident and soaring. Give your soul the attention, discovery, honor, and respect that it deserves. I guarantee that you will prosper from it immensely. Your life will transform from this discovery and connection. Allow yourself the possibility of going deeper, feeling deeper, and knowing deeper. Your soul awaits, savvy?

17

Back to Basics

Let's review a bit, shall we?

Going through a major life overhaul can get you feeling all types of crazy things. "Am I doing it right?" "This is too much for me. Why am I bothering?" You may have so many doubts and concerns, but I'm here to tell you that that's completely normal and okay. We are beings of curiosity *and* comfort. Being outside your comfort zone can be very awkward and difficult, and the need to "get it right" might haunt you. There is no need for that. Your experience, journey, and quest is unique to you, and no one can tell you that you're doing something right or wrong there.

I call this phase of your quest "Back to Basics" because when you are lost, that's all you have to do. You've been given priceless tools to ground you, grow you, and in-lighten you. There is no way you can master these things by doing them only once. They must be practiced consistently and incorporated into your daily life for you to reap the benefits. Go back to them, and use the ones that work for you.

Picture the bumpers on a bowling lane. That's precisely what these tools are for you. They will keep you on track, even when you veer off a little. And with more and more practice and precision, you'll make a strike naturally.

Checkpoint: Backtracking

If you find yourself anxious, nervous, or worried, it's because you've lost your way and/or are veering away from your purpose. Most likely you've been following your body's desires, or you've allowed your mind to run with abandon. What happened to your orientation? Your direction? Your mission?

When this happens, go back to your basics in this book and find the tools you need to get past it. Grounding, meditation, journaling, drawing energy—I've given you an ample number of options. *There are no excuses!*

Caution Bubble

More often than not, our environment or toxic people within our daily grind bring a lot of chaos. Understand that your angst has little to do with your progress. Use your tools! Clear, connect, and feel the force in order to overcome it.

18

Living to Being

A very in-lightened mentor of mine once said, "Living life is complacency. Doing life is living." These impactful words have become a strong motto in my life, as they are quite literally the definition of a complete life's purpose.

The way I see it, three pillars are the makeup of "doing life":

- Your internal life
- Your external life
- Your direction in life

Each of these pillars reflects and supports the other. Balance, grasshopper! They are the foundation to all of your life's experiences—past, present, and future. When these three pillars align, there is strength in all that you are and all that you choose to do. Your energy becomes palpable, and you have purpose, direction, and contentment. Your thoughts, actions, and feelings will obtain a sense of light. With the balance and alignment of these three pillars, you will arrive to an in-lightened state of being.

Your internal life must be studied strategically and meticulously. Having done all of the work and effort that you have so far, this should be a possible task for you. You should now be able to access your purpose with peace of mind, body and soul.

Your external life also must have structure. The structure that you choose is completely up to you, yet it's a structure nonetheless. The effort that you put into yourself determines the greatness that you will receive in life. This is the area where you should stop at nothing, never take no for an answer, and give 100 percent of yourself. Here, you're not living; you're *being*. Be that person—the one you admire, the one who dreams, the one who sets a goal and does everything in his or her power to achieve it, the one who has a sense of fulfillment and accomplishment when his or her head hits the pillow at the end of the day. Breathe it. Be it. *Do it!*

And then there's your direction in life—your purpose, your mission, your bread and butter. I don't feel the need to drill the importance of this more than I already have. This is the sweet spot, the secret to lasting and meaningful happiness. Find out who you are, and do it on purpose. Get it? Got it? Good.

Life happens for us, not to us.
—Tony Robbins

19

Identi-Fly

Having put in a tremendous effort and taken all the steps that Life Quest has guided you through, there is no doubt that you feel and think differently than when you began this journey. The full awareness, knowledge, and miracle that the body, mind, and soul are, are now functioning at a much higher potential for and with you. The word *identify* is rather important in its own right, but with a slight change in spelling to "identi-fly," you can now see the possibility and opportunity that lies at your fingertips.

At this stage you are now able to identi-fly which behaviors work and do not work for you, which lessons you have learned from your past that you wish to repeat or cast aside, and which opportunities you wish to seize, all while accessing the tools of Life Quest to connect and guide you in the process.

Identi-fly your relationships, your work situation, your family life, and so on. Take a good hard look at all that surrounds you, and know with full confidence that you are now connected and able to make decisions that will better you and fulfill your body, mind, and soul. You might have heard the expression, "Show me who your friends are, and I'll tell you who *you* are." This philosophy really does hold true, not only for the people who are consistently in your life but for the situations in which you repeatedly find yourself as well. If any area of your life is not working out to your satisfaction or benefit, you now know the process and have the tools to change it. There is no longer any reason to fly blindly through life and encounter all the chaos that comes with it. Identi-fly your surroundings and maneuver through them in the way that only you can—in an in-lightened state. Identify who you are, what you want, what you stand for, and *fly!*

Checkpoint: The New You
Fill in the blanks, describing the new, empowered person
that you've become.

I am _____

_____

_____

I stand for _____

_____

_____

I am ready to/for _____

_____

_____

20

Love ... Just Love

Love. The epic, ethereal, enigmatic concept that philosophers, scientists, and poets have been trying to describe since the beginning of time. Why is it so important to us? What is it good for? Rather than the *why* or the *what*, let's look at the *how*.

A primary thread runs throughout creation. This energy or light, when vibrating at a high level, will create your highest form of being. Much of your energy is typically focused on the *what*, based in selfish wants and desires. It's living for the self and not recognizing that there is much more to connect to outside of yourself. For example, "What do I want right now?" or "What will make me feel better?" There is no movement in these words, no action. They are stagnant and selfish and a recipe for mediocrity and complacency.

The higher vibration of being on which you should focus is the *how*. "How can I create this?" or "How can I move forward?" These are questions that create, just by being thought or spoken. They set off a chain reaction of motion, action, and results. "The how in the now" should be your predominant thought, now that you're in this new state of being.

Caution Bubble

Let's talk about the gorilla in the room. Most people choose their purpose based on their egos. "I want to be the best, the brightest, the biggest ..." These paths are fueled by selfish or egotistical needs. They lead to a second set of misfired thoughts, such as, "I want the biggest house" or "I want the most expensive car." This doesn't mean you can't or shouldn't enjoy the finer things in life. I am specifically talking about the mindset and attitude that accompanies a low, ego-based vibration. This egocentric existence leads down a path of intolerance, dissatisfaction, and an utter disconnect from a deep and meaningful life. *Stay away!*

Checkpoint: *Goal!*
Write down three of your goals that are based in ego.

1. _____

2. _____

3. _____

Write down three of your goals that are based in love.

1. _____

2. _____

3. _____

Written within your soul's DNA is an experience waiting for you to discover it. It's waiting to be unleashed and lived by you and only you. It's a calling for your mission, for you to be a vehicle of this specific energy of love, not the energy of self-serving. This energy intrigues you and excites you enough to motivate you to make a monumental effort and flourish. Your purpose, your mission, your DNA, your energetic existence, your vibration, your light, and your being is your sustainability. Your life's experiences are gifts that were given to grow you, amplify you, and reinforce your soul. The underlying tone behind all of this, however—behind all of us, for that matter—is the expression of connection, the highest connection naturally being love. Love always, in all ways. Just love ...

Checkpoint 2: Based in Love
What is your life's purpose, based in love?

_____

_____

_____

_____

_____

_____

_____

_____

_____

_____

_____

_____

_____

_____

Set an intention for your life, based in love.

_____

_____

_____

_____

_____

_____

_____

_____

_____

_____

_____

_____

God bless!

21

Notes

(This section is dedicated to your personal thoughts, feelings and growth.)

_____

_____

_____

_____

_____

_____

_____

_____

_____

_____

_____

_____

_____

_____

_____

_____

_____

_____

_____

_____

_____

_____

_____

About the Authors

Morgan Duzoglou

Morgan successfully works as a professional life coach, giving courses and seminars in schools and universities and a character development program in martial arts schools. She also works with private and corporate clients. Her unique experience as a nationally ranked athlete, as well as a recording artist, bring a rare and fresh prospective to the exciting process of self-realization. Morgan is a fifth-degree black belt and holds the title of Sensei, along with several national titles. Her twenty-two-year background in extensively studying and teaching martial arts and its diverse philosophies is what drove Morgan to earn her life coaching degree. Artistry has called to Morgan in many forms; she spent fourteen years in the music industry as a singer/songwriter, contributing her talents to top forty artists in the US Latin market, covering the United States, Latin America, and Europe. Morgan is determined to spread her light and hopes that her unique take on life's journey will touch, transform, and give wondrous possibilities to the lives of others.

Robert Duzoglou

Robert has made searching for excellence and a higher calling an integral part of his personal, work, and family life. He has practiced and taught the enlightened connection that meditation provides for over forty-five years. Robert has reached the highest level that the martial arts have to offer, achieving a tenth-degree black belt, the title of Sensei, and the honor of a place in the Martial Arts Hall of Fame. He has established and run various martial arts academies, resulting in hundreds of black-belt graduates from around the world. Robert's professional business career has included chair of the Coalition of Chambers of Miami Dade, award-winning business banker, real estate developer, and sustainability consultant for several communities throughout the United States. Currently, Robert devotes his time to sustainability engineering and directing his RDCA MMA martial arts program, for which he has grown an incomparable platform with the commendable purpose of influencing, guiding, and instilling values in the youth of today to become the exemplary humans of tomorrow.

Printed in the United States
By Bookmasters